I0493448

Bubba Can Dance
Winning at Work

Randolph A. Pohlman, Ph.D.
Bradley S. Wesner, Ph.D.

First edition published May 2014

For information about special discounts for bulk purchases or about booking the authors as event speakers or trainers, please contact Dr. Wesner at **561-855-0526**. Requests for permission to make copies of any part of this work should also be emailed to: **brad@kbo-consulting.com**

Lyrics to *Shenandoah*'s song, *If Bubba Can Dance (I Can Too)*, were written by Marty Rabon, Mike McGuire, and Bob McDill for RCA in 1993.

Cover Photo: *The Pitbull of Blues Band:* Josh Rowand, Richie Corricelli, Denny Rowand. Find them at *thepitbullofblues.com*

Layout & Design by Trisha Keel
Tomorrow's Key

Manufactured in the United States of America.

1   3   5   7   9   10   8   6   4   2

Pohlman, Ph.D., Randolph A. and Bradley S. Wesner, Ph.D.
Bubba Can Dance – *Winning at Work*

ISBN-13: 978-1499258318
ISBN-10: 1499258313

What Business Leaders Are Saying About...

Bubba Can Dance
Winning *at* Work

"This is a book for everyone at any level in an organization who wants to be successful. It is the basics of blocking and tackling in the work place and will serve those seeking to jump start their career. Read this book and make it happen!"

—*H. Wayne Huizenga,*
Founder of three *Fortune 500* enterprises:
WasteManagement, Blockbuster Video, and AutoNation
Ernst & Young's *Entrepreneur of the Year*, 2008
Previous Owner: Miami Dolphins, Marlins and Florida Panthers

———

"This is the rarest of all business books: an insightful, practical guide to how the working world really works and what it takes to succeed. That's no surprise. The authors are the rarest of all business writers: esteemed academics who also have an uncommon ability to translate the most complex of concepts into understandable language and vivid examples. The end result is a guide that can genuinely help shape careers and drive a more satisfying work life."

—*Mike Jackson,*
Chairman and CEO, AutoNation
Previous President and CEO of Mercedes-Benz USA
Ernst & Young's *Entrepreneur of the Year*, 2011
Fortune Magazine's *Global Business Person of the Year*, 2011

SOCIAL MEDIA SITES

Website: www.Bubba-Can-Dance.com
Facebook: www.facebook.com/BubbaCanDance
LinkedIn: www.linkedin.com/Bubba-Can-Dance
Twitter: www.twitter.com@Bubba-Can-Dance
Tumblr: www.bubba-can-dance.tumblr.com

———

For more about *Shenandoah*,
the band that inspired this book's title,
please visit: http://www.shenandoahband.com

DR. POHLMAN'S DEDICATION

First and foremost I want to thank my wife Jeanne for her support, thoughts and encouragement while I worked on this book. Second I appreciate the encouragement and support of my daughters, Tina and Lisa.

My colleagues at Nova Southeastern University have been generous with their input and support, especially Bahaudin Mujtaba with his insights and thoughtful discussions on many topics we wrote about.

I thank *Shenandoah* for inspiring the title of this book and the helpful discussions with Mike McGuire on the origins of the song and Jim Seales for helping me with the guitar parts (although I assume all responsibility for wrong notes ☺).

I thank the late Paul "Doc" Hersey for being a great friend and mentor who always encouraged and advised me.

My wife and I want to give a special tribute to my administrative assistant of 15 years, the late Linda Rae Hoge, who tirelessly worked on this manuscript up to the time of her death. She was simply the best administrative assistant one could hope for and a great friend!

Finally I want to thank Trisha Keel for her tireless work as an editor with her *get 'er done* attitude.

— *Randolph A. Pohlman*

DR. WESNER'S DEDICATION

To my wonderful wife Kylene for her patience, love, prayer, and hard work in making this book a reality.

To my daughter Anastasia…you are too small to know what daddy is doing right now, but you are the reason I am doing it!

To Cody Lane who taught me more about business and politics than anyone ever has.

To Dr. Cara Jacocks, my fellow warrior in all things academic who pushes me to do more and inspires me at every step.

To Larry and Marcia Wesner, who carried me when I was too weak to go on.

And finally to Richard P. Clemente…you did not live to see it, but you provided inspiration at every step.

God bless you all!

— *Bradley S. Wesner*

Contents

If you want to be successful, it's just this simple:
Know what you are doing.
Love what you are doing.
And believe in what you are doing.

—Will Rogers

INTRODUCTION

WINNING AT WORK

As I began writing this book about how all of us can be more successful at our jobs, the song by *Shenandoah, If Bubba Can Dance (I Can Too)*, kept playing in my head. This great and fun song was written by Marty Rabon, Mike McGuire, and Bob McDill for their second RCA album in 1993, entitled *Under the Kudzu* with Bob McDill.

It is funny and lively, but sends a message that if this person—Bubba—can do something, you can also do it. And, I think all of our mothers told us that at one point or another in our childhood. Here are the words to the song. To get the best effect, get on *YouTube* and watch *Shenandoah* perform it.

> *Well, he saw it on TV and ordered that video*
> *He learned every step at home and never told a soul*
> *When I saw him out there the very first time I knew*
> *Well if Bubba can dance, I can too*

Chorus

> *Well Bubba can scoot, Bubba can slide*
> *Bubba can two step and Bubba can glide*
> *I never thought he had the nerve, he never said a word*
> *Well everybody in the place stand back and give me some*
>   *room*
> *Cause if Bubba can dance, I can too*

> *Now I've been watching all night and I'm working my*
>   *courage up*
> *Hey that dude's on the floor and he's doin' all the latest stuff*
> *Well if he's brave enough then I know what I gotta do*
> *Hey if Bubba can dance, I can too*

Chorus

> *Well if Bubba can dance, I can too*
> *Well if Bubba can dance, I can too*

This song, though much fun, says a lot. If you are willing to work hard, learn a skill, and have the right personality for the work you too can be successful! And sometime in our lives we have looked at the *Bubba's* out there in our world and wondered how they did it. What really made that guy so successful? What got her that promotion? And maybe the most important question of all: What makes that person different then me? In a very real way, that is what this book is about. We are going to identify those things that make people successful at work and cultivate them in YOU.

So, let's get to work on being successful at what we do. After all, if Bubba can do it—you can too!

CHAPTER 1

SUCCESS FACTORS

Much has been written about getting rich, investing for big returns, having your own business, working at home, and the importance of exercise and diet for a better life. There is nothing wrong with any of these concepts and many of them can be much to your benefit. Yet for most of us, our immediate concerns of success are a bit more basic. In short, we spend an enormous amount of time at work. This profoundly affects our lives. So a major question for all of us, at any level, is: "What will make us the most successful in our job?" Regardless of what our job is, there are factors common to all jobs that can greatly enhance our success at work.

You might ask, "Isn't my job in marketing very different than a person's job in a comparable level in the information technology area of my firm? How could there be common factors for our job success?" Clearly there are differences in knowledge, skills, and abilities for one job compared to the other. However there are just as many, if not more, characteristics or behaviors that are necessary and common to both jobs. We call these *success factors*. They are the basic qualities that lead to success in any position—including yours!

A great deal has been written about leadership and management, but little of consequence has been written to help the typical person become more successful at work. What makes a person successful in the work place? Is it pure skill; is it personality, the ability to cope with organizational politics or just plain old hard work? In this book, we will find out just what it takes to be successful in the workplace.

We all know people who lack one attribute needed for success and possess all of the others. These people often fail to ever come close to realizing their potential due to their own deficiencies. These individuals have talent but waste massive amounts of time, energy, and effort resulting from their lack of understanding and inability to correct these deficiencies. These workers have the ability to cultivate success. All they need to do is understand the success factors which will overcome their deficiencies, and all of their hard work will finally pay off. As we will see, skills get you so far, but they do not get you all the way.

Most of us are not afraid to invest in skills and equipment to enhance our abilities outside of work. People spend tons of money on golf and tennis lessons, fishing gear, boats, cycling, etc., but how much do they invest in helping themselves succeed in the workplace? The answer is, unfortunately, almost nothing. Why? The reason is that it is not always clear what one must do to be successful in the workplace, nor, once this knowledge is gained, how to put those skills to use immediately.

We also have some societal issues that must be overcome. There is a culture in this country that believes employers should provide the training for employees and it is their duty and obligation to do so if they want employees to perform well. Guess what? It is YOUR responsibility *as a person*, not as an employee, to make yourself as good in the workplace as possible to benefit not only your employer, but also yourself and your family. Too many people have silently developed this entitlement mentality and most of them do not even know it! This entitlement mentality is so frequently reinforced in our society that we do not even recognize it any more. You know the old saying, "There are those who make things happen, those who watch things happen and those who wonder what happened"? MAKE THINGS HAPPEN FOR YOURSELF!

Let's consider a professional example. Does Bubba Watson practice, work on various parts of his game and conditioning, sign autographs, give frequent interviews, and do such a great job with commercials and fans just to satisfy his "employer"? No! Bubba knows that to be successful he must be good at a lot of things, and many of them take hard work, patience, etc., as well as his God-given gift of natural talent. Whose responsibility is it to keep him at the top of his game? The PGA? No! It is Bubba's responsibility. By taking on the job himself, Bubba determines his own destiny on the links and works to the maximum of his potential (RP). *[Each author's initials will come after the examples so you'll know which of us is writing where, (RP) for Randolph Pohlman, and (BW) for Bradley Wesner.]*

It is time for YOU to take charge of your workplace success, which will result in less stress, more money, a better working environment, more happiness and security for you and your family, and more success for your employer. If you respond that you do not want to make your employer better off, you are with the wrong organization, or you need a major attitude adjustment! However, if you are ready to make an investment in your own work success, keep reading!

In your organization, what happens if someone is not doing their job, or part of their job, for any reason? Someone else has to pick up the slack. Right? If this occurs, then the person who picks up the slack most likely doesn't have time to do all of his or her own work. This scenario is all too common in today's workplace. An extreme example of this is a great brain surgeon who has someone to clean up the operating room, sterilize all the instruments, etc. Let us assume for a minute that the brain surgeon does just as excellent a job as the professional who normally cleans up the operating room. Should the surgeon spend his time cleaning up the operating room, or should he allow the professional already assigned the task to attend to cleaning the operating room? You would answer: certainly the doctor should let the other person do it. It would be foolish for him to spend all of his time or much of his time cleaning up the operating room. Why? Because the surgeon adds great value to the organization and to society by doing surgery—not cleaning up the operating room and instruments. Someone with a different sort of training could do an excellent job of cleaning, even though they are unable to perform surgeries.

However, let's draw on this example a bit further. One undeniable fact is that the operation room and instruments must be clean and sterilized. This is essential for the surgeon to perform optimally and with minimal risk to the patient he will serve. In the event that the person tasked with attending to the operating

Bubba Can Dance

room does not complete their job or does a poor job, the room must still be attended. This forces someone, potentially even the surgeon himself, to do it. This is true for any position within any organization. If we fail to complete tasks as assigned, we simply make more work for someone above us to do, and in the process we utilize their higher level of skills poorly. The result is efficiency loss within the organization. So consider this: Have you ever done a poor job, or only a partial job which you have been asked to do? Be honest with yourself.

Now personalize the example a bit more. Imagine for a moment that you could have a one-time meeting with a business titan like Warren Buffett, Bill Gates, Wayne Huizenga, or Jack Welch. If one of these successful people came to a place where you could interact with them, would you want to meet them? Why? You probably responded like most people do—*Well, they have done so much, accomplished so much, and made so much money that I could learn a lot from them, and that might be valuable to me and my career.*

Let's now ask more questions. Why would *they* want to meet you? What do you bring to the table, what can they learn from you, how can you help them? The fact is that people want to be around others who can make a valuable contribution in business and, in fact, to life in general. In other words, successful people learn constantly, and draw value, from those around them. So, what do you bring to the table right now? What can you develop? With this book you will find answers those questions.

The purpose of this book is to help everyone from top management to the lowest-paid employee in an organization understand the fundamentals for success in the workplace. To make this happen, this book creates a common language for discussions among employees and employers, in and outside of their work environments, allowing them to begin to understand, communicate, and reinforce the success factors. This common language will allow all employees, from management all the way down to the lowest-paid employee, to have a clear and common understanding of the importance of these factors in the workplace. It is a case where everyone wins!

The importance of opening the lines of communication between levels of management cannot be overstated, and is fundamental to becoming successful. I personally have witnessed countless examples of barriers to advancement being overcome rapidly with efforts being made to simply *talk to the boss*. Within this book we will reference communication at almost every step. Further, we will dedicate an entire chapter to the concept.

Remember, this book is for you—not someone else. It is designed specifically to help individuals—YOU—improve in the workplace. In many cases this is going to require a change in the way you think, act, and communicate. Reading, understanding, and following the advice in this book can help you become much more successful in the workplace, significantly reduce your stress, increase your earning capacity, and, in general, help make life much more enjoyable and lead to long-term happiness.

We will talk about eleven behaviors essential for success in the workplace. Each chapter will cover one specific behavior, what it means, why it is important to you, give you examples of good and bad behavior, and provide a place for you to begin your plans to improve your behavior in this area.

The chapters are not placed in order of importance—they are

all very important! They are also designed so that you can read the book from beginning to end, or rush to a section most important to you today. Additionally, there is a place for you to keep a personal journal of your success in altering your behavior to become more successful in the workplace.

The heart of this book focuses eleven chapters on ways to help you with specific behaviors. Each of those chapters stems from the same three fundamentals:

1. You must have skills, knowledge, the ability to apply them, and the talent to communicate your knowledge to those around you.

2. You must have a strong work ethic.

3. You must have a personality that people will want to work with.

Keep these fundamentals in mind as you proceed.

Remember, this book is for YOU—for your personal improvement. It is not intended to be a general book to read and put back on your bookshelf. It is one you can take personally to observe your own behaviors relative to the behaviors specified to make you successful and begin to make modifications in these behaviors to become much more effective in the workplace.

Here is how the book will work. Each chapter has:

*   Explanations and discussions of the concept
*   Examples of good and bad behaviors
*   Self test of your behaviors
*   Evaluating matrix to calculate a score of your behaviors
*   Plan for self-improvement
*   Journal of successes and lapses

You must commit to improvement if you are in fact going to improve. Just like a diet to lose weight where you just can't read about the diet and lose—you can't just read this book and improve! To be more successful at your job you must commit to improvement and work at it. Take the time to date, add your name and read aloud the pledge that follows. Sign it with conviction and you will significantly improve your success in the workplace!

Personally, I find that when I seek to make a change in my personal or professional life, that a major key to sticking with it is making it official. Nothing is more official than putting your commitment in writing, so at this time we offer you the opportunity to make this pledge official and put it in writing. This is the first step to *your new commitment to success*.

My Pledge to Myself

Today, _____ ,

I, _____ ,

pledge to myself to observe and understand my behaviors

which affect my work. I pledge to significantly improve

them, which will greatly improve my success in the

workplace, enhance my earning power, help me accumulate

wealth, live much more stress-free, and enjoy my life more.

Bubba can dance—and *I can too!*

Signed _____

A man only learns in two ways:
one by reading,
and the other,
by association with smarter people.

—*Will Rogers*

CHAPTER 2 - ACQUIRING AND USING KNOWLEDGE and SKILLS

What do we mean by the acquiring and applying of knowledge and skills? The first part is very simple. How much knowledge have you acquired? Or more simply stated, What do you know that is valuable to an employer? What do you bring to the party? We are not talking about the number of certificates you have or the number of courses or seminars you have sat (or slept) through.

What we are talking about is how much knowledge and how many skills you have that are directly useful in the workplace. If you have responded, "I don't have that many because my employer has not provided them for me," you are on the wrong track.

Let us make it perfectly clear from the very beginning. It is YOUR responsibility to gain knowledge. You must take the initiative to seek this education or knowledge—even if you have to go outside the organization to get it and pay for it yourself!

Why? Because your personal success, wealth, and happiness

depend upon it! Put simply, if you are reading this book, success matters to you. Acquiring skills and knowledge that enhance your skill set allows you to be instrumental in the success of the organization and yourself. This is an important concept, and one that has recently been shrouded in misperceptions.

Oftentimes, people complain about how much a doctor, lawyer, certified mechanic, or plumber charges. The fact of the matter is, all these professionals, as well as many others, have a great deal of knowledge gained through education, training, and experience which allows them to be very good at their job. Professional services are fairly costly because the costs that these individuals expended during the years they spent in schooling and learning their profession need to be recovered.

Further, not everyone has the skills in question. After all if we could unstop the drain ourselves we wouldn't have called a plumber! Yet, these skilled individuals have taken it upon themselves to acquire relatively rare skills that, once developed to a level of excellence, people are willing to pay for. In each case, these individuals have dedicated long hours and countless dollars toward perfecting their craft and, for the most part, have done so on their own initiative.

What does this mean to you? Let us establish one fact right now: It is YOUR responsibility, no one else's, to increase your knowledge and be able to use it. This is not to say the employer has no responsibility, but then we go down a road that leads us to a situation where we are completely dependent upon others because you have an entitlement mentality. For you to be successful, you must take charge of your life and the acquisition of knowledge to enhance your life in the workplace.

In the broader sense, this concept is often referred to as ***Locus of Control***, which has two dimensions: internal and external. People with an *Internal Locus of Control* feel as if THEY are in charge of what happens in their life. People with an *External Locus of Control* feel like outside forces determine everything. A person with an external locus of control is like a small figure of a man sitting on a bench who looks up at the bird perched above him and says, "Go ahead—everyone else does."

In contrast, a person with an internal locus of control looks at the bird, realizes what is going to happen, and then moves so he doesn't get hit. In other words, having an internal locus of control means we take charge of our own outcomes.

So, now let's assess your knowledge of your organization. Ask yourself what kind of knowledge you have of the organization you work for.

- Do you see the big picture?
- Do you know what the organization is about?
- Do you know what its objectives are?
- Do you pay attention to its mission statement?
- Are you really knowledgeable of the company, its products and services?
- What kind of technical skills do you have related to your job?
- Do you have the highest level of technical skills that you can personally obtain for your job?
- Are your skills in the top 10% of your peers?
- Is your ability to apply your skills in the top 10% of your peers?

To be successful with this book you must be brutally honest

with yourself. This is not intended to put yourself down, but to be open to improving. Nearly everyone you will meet who has been successful or has achieved greatness continually strives to improve.

The second aspect of being able to gain the most out of your knowledge is being able to apply it. We have all been around people who know a huge amount about their work, but do not know how to apply it to be successful. So, the second portion of this chapter is focused on the application of knowledge because if you cannot apply it, it is not going to help you in the workplace. Ask yourself:

- Do you frequently think about your work and what knowledge and skills you have or need and how you may be able to better understand and apply them in your job?
- Are you willing to share your knowledge?
- Can you teach others?
- Can you coach others to help improve the quality of the work in the organization?

Let's look at a couple of examples. Consider Mary, a young middle manager who I worked with while performing a leadership seminar at her company. Mary struggled with public speaking and knew that she needed to improve her presentation skills to move forward in the organization. At the conclusion of my seminar, she approached me and informed me of her challenge. I was eager to help. I was so intrigued by her problem that I even offered to help her free of charge. All that she had to do was email me and set an appointment.

Three months went by and Mary never made contact. I was a bit confused until I returned to the organization for another seminar and happened to run into her. Her situation had not changed.

She still struggled with public speaking and had done nothing to correct the problem. When I asked her why she had not taken me up on my offer of free help, her response demonstrated the essence of an external locus of control. Mary informed me that she had approached her supervisor for time off to meet with me for the training in question. Her supervisor had informed her that, due to a pending project, it was not a good time for her to be off. Mary looked at this decision as "her boss keeping her down."

She abandoned trying to correct her skill set and settled for staying in her current state of mediocrity. Even though I had offered to provide the training on her day off, Mary considered that time hers and believed that if the organization wanted her to have presentation skills that those skills should be attained on the clock.

In this situation, Mary views her training as something that her organization should provide. In other words, they have to take the initiative to provide her skills. And, if they do not do so, for any reason, Mary's response is to throw up her hands and quit. Even if acquiring excellent presentation skills would result in her promotion, Mary refuses to take the initiative herself (BW).

Now let's consider Rick Jones of Rick Jones' Pianos. As Rick's website says, he has the "Largest, coolest piano warehouse on planet Earth." Who taught Rick about pianos? How did he acquire his skills and apply them? Well, it all started very modestly when Rick's father suggested he learn how to tune pianos because of his natural ability to fix things (lawn mowers, washers, grandfather clocks, etc.). He attended Shenandoah Conservatory of Music and left when he thought he had what he needed to go out and use it. He worked at rebuilding shops for five years while tuning pianos at home on the side. He started his own piano business in 1983 out of his house and still tuned pianos at people's houses on the side. Eventually he moved to a slightly larger store then finally to the current location with a 35,000 square foot warehouse with an average of 250 pianos in stock.

Did someone spoon feed Rick to give him the skills, knowledge and the ability to apply it? NO! Rick had, and has, an internal locus of control. He took control of his own destiny by recognizing his existing ability and then working to acquire additional skills. He busted his tail for years working seven days a week to gain the skills, knowledge, and the ability to apply them. He spent his own money and time to learn and perfect his craft (RP).

Here is a little test to better evaluate your technical skills and your understanding of the big picture of your company, as well as understand your ability to apply them. In this and all the following Calculation charts, rate each category with a score of 1–5, with 5 being the highest.

Bubba Can Dance

MY SKILL & KNOWLEDGE CALCULATION

Identify skill or knowledge needed for your work	Identify skill or knowledge level you have (Rate 1–5)	Ability to effectively use skill and knowledge (Rate 1–5)	TOTAL SCORE	Importance of skill or knowledge to your job performance (Rate 1–5)

If there is a skill or knowledge in the first column that you rate high on in your second and third columns, and it's very important to you, that's great! If you don't rate very high on your level of skills or knowledge, but it is very important to your work then, like Bubba, you better order the video and get to work. This means you need to get to work as soon as possible to acquire this skill or knowledge and learn to apply it!

For the best results, write out your answers to the following Self Assessment questions.

SELF ASSESSMENT

1. Do I understand the big picture of my job and the company for which I work? _____

    _____

    _____

2. What is the big picture of my job? _____

    _____

    _____

3. What is the big picture of the company? _____

    _____

    _____

4. The behaviors I need to modify to improve my technical skills and my big picture skills and my ability to apply them within the organization. _____

    _____

    _____

5. Behaviors I need to modify: First Example—Get more specific training or education and be able to apply it to the workplace. Second Example—Be more engaged in the company's mission. List your change goals here: _____

    _____

    _____

    _____

HOW TO USE THIS SECTION

This is your personal journal. Keep it private. Track your progress as you date the action behaviors that you changed. The ratings are intended to be for your self-evaluation, not for your boss or anyone else. This is your personal journal to track how you expand your personal responsibility to modify your behaviors so you will be more successful in the workplace.

If your employer has a plan, and you work that out, that is fine—and actually should be encouraged—but work on your own as well. Be honest with yourself about how you stand with regard to where you need to be with your technical and big picture skills and their application in the workplace.

PERSONAL IMPROVEMENT PLAN

WEAKNESSES	CORRECTIVE ACTIONS	EXPECTED OUTCOMES

JOURNAL: HOW AM I DOING? *(IN YOUR OWN OPINION)*

1. _____

_____

_____

2. _____

_____

_____

3. _____

_____

_____

4. _____

_____

_____

5. _____

_____

_____

6. _____

_____

_____

TIPS:

- Be tenacious about learning more technical skills. Read about them in trade magazines, on the Internet, etc.

- Think about how to improve your technical skills when you have spare time (rather than watch TV or browsing the Internet all evening)

- Read and think about how you apply your skills.

- Read and learn all you can about the organization you work for:

  ○ What does the organization do?

  ○ What is their mission?

  ○ What is the strategic plan for the organization?

In the long run, we shape our lives,
and we shape ourselves.
The process never ends until we die.
And the choices we make
are ultimately our own responsibility.

—*Eleanor Roosevelt*

Bubba Can Dance

CHAPTER 3

RESPONSIBILITY: Making it Personal

Taking responsibility for your success so that the organization can reach its goals is a major factor in cultivating your success in the workplace. What do we mean by responsibility? Responsibility means that you accept accountability and perform without your supervisor telling you to. Responsibility means that you take the initiative when something needs to be done and you will not let it pass without getting it done—and done correctly. There is a great book I would recommend to all of you entitled, *Taking Responsibility: Self-Reliance and the Accountable Life*, by Nathaniel Branden, which explains in great detail what it means to take responsibility.

This section is about is taking responsibility for all of your actions and all of the expectations placed upon you while seeking the best possible result. We have all seen people who take on an extremely high level of responsibility, and, no matter what happens, they take it upon themselves to get things done. These people take so much pride in their work that they will not permit anything or anyone involved with their project to fail.

On the other hand, we all know people who are so irresponsible that if they are given a task and are unable to accomplish it, they simply shrug their shoulders and do not worry about being accountable for the lack of results. They do minimal work, never put their hearts into their work, and they take little or no pride in outcomes with which they are associated. In other words, they do the job *good enough* and work just hard enough to make sure that they won't get fired.

As you can see very quickly, the differences between these two perspectives of responsibility are critical to determining your success in the workplace. Irresponsible people in the workplace go nowhere and end up working in the same position for their entire career while wondering why fortune never smiled on them with a promotion. In contrast, those who embrace personal responsibility for their actions and take a personal stake in their work product are much more likely to advance quickly to ever greater responsibility and success.

Take the example of Myrna being asked to prepare name tags for attendees at a major corporate event. Myrna knew that the event included 400 people but received a list of only 230 names. Myrna, not being a responsible person, just took the 230 names and made name tags with no consideration of the other 170 people who were attending the event. After all, in her opinion, if her boss wanted her to do the job it was his responsibility to provide a complete list.

As a result the evening of the event came with a shortage of 170 name tags. Furthermore, Myrna did not think to bring a computer and material to make extras on the spot. The result—a disaster and a lot of upset customers!

What would she have done if she were a responsible employee? Simple! She would have assumed responsibility for the success of the event and the reputation of organization. Being responsible means taking full accountability for a situation with no excuses. As Larry the Cable Guy would say, "Just get 'er done!" Or, as we often said in the military when asked why we did not accomplish something, "No excuse, Sir."

Take the case of Robert, who was asked to call three specific people to get their thoughts on whether to go ahead with a very important project. Robert made calls to two of these individuals but they did not return his phone calls. What should he have done? First of all he should have called all three individuals not just two! Secondly he should have made follow-up phone calls. Did Robert take responsibility for getting the information he was supposed to get? NO! He made a feeble attempt then abandoned his responsibility (RP).

In contrast, consider the following. Some friends and I, seven of us in all, were out for a guys' night on the town in a major city. We decided to visit a favorite high-end steak house for dinner. As we looked at the menu we arrived at a common decision without discussing it: We all decided to have the T-bone steak. Our server, Linda, took our order and delivered it to the kitchen. Upon returning with our meal, she delivered each T-bone to its owner until she arrived to the last steak—mine.

She quietly placed a filet in front of me. Before I could even formulate my complaint, Linda spoke. She said, "I want to personally apologize. When I delivered the order to the chef, we miscounted and the chef only prepared six T-bones. We realized this and quickly prepared a filet for you so that you would not be the only person at the table not eating. Please accept this filet, and our most sincere apologies. Naturally, your T-bone is being prepared right now and will be out in a moment."

It was. My T-bone arrived in less than two minutes. Linda was not going to allow the organization to fail over a mistake. She took responsibility and made it personal. I later found out how personal: Linda paid for my dinner that night out of her own pocket. Naturally, I have been back to that restaurant countless times. Linda now runs it. Is there any wonder why? (BW)

As you can see, taking responsibility is crucial to your success. You must be honest with yourself as to whether you are a person of accountability. Are you always seeking responsibility, or are you the type that shrugs your shoulders and does not really care? If you are in the latter group, you can be assured that you will not be successful in the workplace over the long haul! Instead be like Linda. Take responsibility to the highest level you can to make your work excellent. Make it personal and know that the organization's reputation rests on your shoulders, and with its success you will find success yourself.

So, take a moment to consider your own perception of responsibility. Complete the Assignment chart. Then consider the following Self Assessment questions and write out your answers.

HOW RESPONSIBLE AM I? (RATE 1–5, 5 is highest)

List five assignments and rate the level of responsibility you took:

Assignment	Rating

SELF ASSESSMENT

1. Where, in the last six months, have I shown great levels of responsibility?_____

   _____

   _____

   _____

2. Where, in the last six months, have I failed to take responsibility that, in retrospect, I should have taken?____

   _____

   _____

   _____

3. Why did I fail to take responsibility in these areas?_____

   _____

   _____

   _____

Bubba Can Dance

MY RESPONSIBILITY CALCULATION

My work responsibilities	My rating (1–5)	Importance to my work (Rate 1–5)	Total Score (Add columns and compare to 10 total)

PERSONAL IMPROVEMENT PLAN

WEAKNESSES	CORRECTIVE ACTIONS	EXPECTED OUTCOMES

Bubba Can Dance

JOURNAL: HOW AM I DOING? *(IN YOUR OWN OPINION)*

1. _____

_____

_____

2. _____

_____

_____

3. _____

_____

_____

4. _____

_____

_____

5. _____

_____

_____

6. _____

_____

_____

TIPS:

- Always arrive to work ready to take responsibility and —
  that means getting there in time to be prepared to actually
  work at designated starting time.

- Always finish projects early. Remember Murphy's Law:
  If something can go wrong, it will. Start early and plan to
  finish early so any crisis that comes up (work or personal)
  cannot interfere with getting the assignment completed.

- If someone else drops the ball, pick up the slack. It may
  frustrate or irritate you at the time, but the truth will be
  revealed at some point and you will get a reputation for
  being a winner.

- Own everything you do. Make sure everything you do is
  done with excellence.

- Take pride in your workplace. Take care of office
  equipment, furniture, and facilities—as if it is your own. It
  is your home away from home.

CHAPTER 4

PUNCTUALITY

What do we mean by punctuality and how important is it? Punctuality means getting to work on time and things done on time. This includes being at your job and ready to go, on or before your time to start. As William Shakespeare said, "Better three hours too soon than a minute too late."

We often hear from the younger workers who say, "What difference does it make if I arrive ten to fifteen minutes late, thirty minutes, or even an hour late? What is important is that I get my job done."

In most work cultures, this is not going to work! The reason may have nothing to do with whether you get your job done. What it does involve is the perception others have of you, and that perception has repercussions for your success.

Coming to work late conveys a message that, "I have more important things to do." Now, that may not be what you intended to communicate at all, but that IS what people think. The truth is that we all have more important things than work, but not when it is time to work!

Punctuality affects people's perception of your work ethic: your attitude, passion, and dedication to your work. If you do not have a good attitude toward work, passion for what you do, and a dedication to your job, you must find a job that you do have a passion for and can dedicate yourself to which will bring out the best attitude and work ethic in you. It is your responsibility to find this job. Consider your attitude toward punctuality for a moment. What is it saying about you? What is it saying about your job choice?

A good example of punctuality that I see in the workplace is a band called *Thunderhead*. They are always punctual. They either start on time or early. They do their work—playing, singing, and performing—with passion, a strong work ethic, and a great attitude. If the band feels that they need to keep playing (working) to hold the crowd and keep them there for the remainder of the evening, they keep playing. I have seen them play (work) for two hours or longer, all in one set (a normal set is 40 minutes playing with a 20-minute break).

On the other hand, I see many groups performing that start late, play very long songs, take a break, and then try to stretch out their break for as long as possible. In other words, they do not look like they want to work. They only want to get paid. They care little about their customers other than that they buy a ticket. Over time, this disrespectful and unprofessional reputation catches up with them and impacts their success (RP).

We all know fellow employees who come in late, take every

break possible, are not punctual with work assignments, and the only thing they are punctual about is going home at the end of the day. If a project is due on a certain date, they want to delay it to a future date to have more time—every time. They create an expectation of lateness in the hopes of normalizing it with those they work with. What they succeed in doing is guaranteeing eventual employment and advancement problems.

Assume you are the boss and you always get in around 7:00 am. You make a practice of taking a short break at around 8:30 am when everyone is expected to be at their workstation. You look out the window and see people sauntering in at 8:45 with a cup of coffee in hand and no hurry in their walk. What would your opinion be about these laggards? Not good!

Then there is the case of the president of the company who is always late for appointments—often 30 minutes to an hour late. He really never says much about it or apologizes for it. Others can only guess that it is just because he is the boss and no one else's time is worth as much as his.

This shows an enormous unawareness and a tremendous lack of regard for other people. In short, it is just rude and disrespectful to others. If you are a *boss* at any level, don't do it! Many bosses approach me asking why their employees fail to take them seriously, communicate openly, or fail to buy into the organizational mission. In many cases the root cause of these problems is a perception that the boss is disconnected from the needs and considerations of the staff. Bosses who fail to be punctual when their employees are counting on them often perpetuate that perception, and this is something that bosses everywhere need to correct today.

Consider this real world example. I recently worked with a client named Anitra, a middle manager at a major insurance company. Anitra reported that she had major problems with employee morale and quite a problem with turnover. She hired me to determine the source of the problem. As I worked with her for a number of months, I noticed a pattern that caused me some concern. During the first four days of the week, Anitra and her staff worked like a Swiss watch. However, when Friday arrived the mood of the office changed dramatically. People became cranky from the start of the day, and throughout the day their attitudes continued to deteriorate. Over the months I was with them, I determined the source of the problem: *The Friday Meeting*.

Anitra had a standing meeting with her team at 3:00 pm on Fridays. The problem was that she would normally meet with her superiors at 2:00 pm on Friday, and that meeting would often run long, or Anitra would run behind in preparing her notation for the 3:00 meeting. In either instance, the perception of her team when she arrived 15-45 minutes late was horrible. They assumed that she simply did not care about their interests and, in particular, they believed that she did not care if they got to leave on time on Friday afternoon. The result of her lateness was a perception of perpetual disrespect that was often reflected in the attitude of her staff. In the end we addressed her punctuality at the Friday meeting and in doing so corrected the morale and turnover issues almost instantly (BW).

What is your work environment like? Is it okay to come in late? Does everyone else come in late too? Have you ever been late for no good reason? Discuss this with your colleagues. What do they think about being punctual? Write out your answers.

SELF ASSESSMENT

1. Are you always ready to do your job on time or early? Why or why not? _____

   _____

   _____

2. Do you complete projects on time or before? Why or why not? _____

   _____

   _____

   _____

3. Are you prompt in responding to requests? Why or why not? _____

   _____

   _____

   _____

4. Do you return e-mails or calls in a timely manner? Why or why not? _____

   _____

   _____

   _____

5. Are you always on time and well prepared for meetings? Why or why not?_____

   _____

   _____

   _____

MY PUNCTUALITY CALCULATION

Things I must be punctual for	My rating (1-5)	Importance to my work (Rate 1-5)	TOTAL SCORE (Add columns and compare to 10 possible)

Bubba Can Dance

PERSONAL IMPROVEMENT PLAN

WEAKNESSES	CORRECTIVE ACTIONS	EXPECTED OUTCOMES

JOURNAL: HOW AM I DOING? *(IN YOUR OWN OPINION)*

1. _____

_____

_____

2. _____

_____

_____

3. _____

_____

_____

4. _____

_____

_____

5. _____

_____

_____

6. _____

_____

_____

TIPS:

- Always be to work on time (this means being at your work station ready to work—not just driving into the parking lot or walking through the front door).

- Always finish projects on time.

- If you have direct reports or indirect reports, make sure they follow the first tip.

- When assessing how long it will take you to complete a project, be sure to be realistic and do not give yourself too little time.

- Build into projects time for mistakes, delays, etc. (They will happen).

- Never wait until the last minute—invariably a snag will occur and you will find yourself behind.

Beginning today, treat everyone you meet
as if they were going to be dead by midnight.
Extend to them all the care, kindness and
understanding you can muster, and
do it with no thought of any reward.

Your life will never be the same again.

—*Og Mandino*

CHAPTER 5

COLLEGIALITY

What is collegiality, and why is it important? Collegiality is your ability to get along well with others and handle your responsibilities, and it is fundamental to your success at work. Most successful people in the workplace are those whom other colleagues like to work with.

Think of your workplace and who you work with on a daily basis. Think about those people you like to work with, who you seek out for camaraderie to take breaks with, to seek advice from, and who are truly enjoyable to be around. These are good colleagues.

A comment often heard in the workplace is that, "Yes, I know she is smart and she knows a lot about the job, but I don't like working with her. She just isn't a good colleague." In a survey taken from participants in a focus group done by the author (Pohlman) and the president of a major American company to see what impeded work the most in the workplace, the lack of collegiality was repeatedly the number one reason!

The causes of poor collegiality can be numerous. Some people have health problems that have a major impact on their collegiality. Some encounter physical problems that lower their tolerance to others. If you have ever had a bad headache at work, you know what this feels like. Imagine if those headaches represented a chronic condition. Still others may face mental health problems that impinge on their collegiality. Family lives may cause a great deal of stress that impairs collegiality. The environment in which people grow up can affect their collegiality. Some people are shy and others are outgoing. Some people are very giving and others are very selfish. Some like to fit in and others do not want to fit in at all.

Prejudice, stereotypes and preconceived notions about groups of people can create great difficulties with collegiality. Usually when two people with diverse backgrounds who may be cautious toward one another get to know each other on a personal level, the stereotypes or prejudices go away.

The case of poor collegiality is one of the most difficult problems to overcome due to the fact that supervisors and those supervised do not like to talk about the lack of collegiality. It is hard for supervisors to pinpoint and give examples that are definitive enough to employees to be helpful and vise versa. Those accused of not being "collegial" are often defensive in these discussions and after the discussion, put the blame on other people or against the employer.

A good way to see how collegiality affects the workplace is to imagine that in your workplace you are very dependent upon the information/technology staff, but you are not a very collegial person. You are often offensive with your remarks, complaining about their service, and generally creating a negative feeling with them about you and your part of the organization. Rightly or wrongly, don't you think that this is going to greatly affect how responsive they are to you, and how helpful (or not helpful) they are in getting problems resolved? It is just human nature that people like to help those who are cordial, friendly, helpful, and treat other people well. When you have a problem with your computer and it seems that IT just cannot get to you for a few days, you are feeling the backlash for your lack of collegiality.

Do not mistake just being quiet or shy for poor collegiality. Take the case of Jon who is very shy but a kind, giving, and fun person when he gets to know you. People mistake Jon for an unfriendly, stuck-up person. People don't invite him to parties or try to fit him with the group. Finally, someone gets to know Jon by chance and tells all the others what a great guy Jon is and what he is really like!

In contrast, take Albert. On the surface he seems collegial, but in working with him you see that he is very negative, suspicious of others, and offensive to many people. His supervisors have discussed this with him numerous times. They write it up in his evaluations, but Albert just doesn't get it! He thinks he just speaks his mind and "gets along" with others just fine. The problem here is people like Albert think all others are wrong and don't realize others avoid them whenever possible but are cordial to him when they can't—which he interprets as collegiality.

Take the case of Beatrice who appears friendly but always has something negative to say about everyone. It is hard to understand why some people do this. It seems that they just can't help it;

they must say something negative about others with little or no prompting required from others. This behavior always leads one to wonder, *When I leave, what do they say about me?* This is a very bad habit to get into. If you do this, STOP!

Shelly is another with a collegiality problem. The old saying applies to Shelly that "If you ask her what time it is, she will tell you how to make a watch!" Shelly thinks she is collegial, but people cringe when they see her coming because they know she will start talking and then go on for what seems an eternity. She also constantly takes personal calls on her cell phone, which probably takes 30% of her work time. (I know, her supervisor should make her stop, but she doesn't.) Her behavior frustrates and irritates others around her in the workplace, and hence her collegiality—not to mention her productivity—suffers.

Then there is Mark who is very friendly, helpful and a great deal of fun to work with. Everyone considers him very collegial. But often he misses or nearly misses deadlines, putting a lot of stress on coworkers. As a result, this creates havoc for other colleagues. By most measures Mark is considered collegial, but his working habits are detrimental to his overall collegiality because he sometimes hampers other workers.

You know what you need to do be handle your responsibilities and get along with your co-workers. Be the kind of colleague *you* want to work with. Respect the work, the workers and the workplace. Use forethought and be considerate. Do your best.

So, let's take a moment to consider your own perception of collegiality. Consider the following questions and write out your answers.

SELF ASSESSMENT

1. Are you collegial? Why or why not? _____

    _____

    _____

    _____

2. Do people seem to like to be around you? Why do you think they do or do not? _____

    _____

    _____

    _____

3. Do others seek you out to have lunch or for a break? Why do you think they do or do not? _____

    _____

    _____

    _____

4. Does my supervisor compliment me on my collegiality? Why do you think they do or do not? _____

    _____

    _____

    _____

5. Would really prefer to not deal with the people you work with? Why or why not? _____

    _____

    _____

    _____

MY COLLEGIAL SKILLS CALCULATION

Where in my work can I be collegial?	My rating (1–5)	Importance to my work (Rate 1–5)	TOTAL SCORE (Each one will calculate and compare differently)

Bubba Can Dance

PERSONAL IMPROVEMENT PLAN

WEAKNESSES	CORRECTIVE ACTIONS	EXPECTED OUTCOMES

JOURNAL: HOW AM I DOING? *(IN YOUR OWN OPINION)*

1. _____
_____
_____

2. _____
_____
_____

3. _____
_____
_____

4. _____
_____
_____

5. _____
_____
_____

6. _____
_____
_____

TIPS:

- Do not take yourself too seriously. If you have a big ego, lose it.

- Always take the high road in disagreements. You can disagree without being disagreeable.

- Do not participate in gossip.

- Try to help others when possible.

- Always stay positive in your outlook.

- Encourage your colleagues and supervisor whenever possible and appropriate.

- Avoid complaining about anything, ever. Focus instead on solutions.

Facts from paper are not the same
as facts from people.

The reliability of the people giving you the facts
is as important as the facts themselves.

—Harold S. Geneen

CHAPTER 6

RELIABILITY

Reliability is being able to be counted on to do the right things correctly and within a given time frame. Are you reliable? *Business Week*, in its February 19, 2008 issue, covered a story about why most CEOs get fired. The answer is, they do not get things done. In other words, one of the things they are *not* is reliable. Making claims about vision and change is one thing, but actually being able to get an organization to realize your vision is quite another.

In business, we all want to be able to count on things being done in a timely manner, with appointments and responsibilities met on time. Many of you may have experienced a lack of reliability with your cable company. I did recently! My cable company told me that they would be at my house between 4:00 pm and 7:00 pm to make a repair. Mind you, I was getting ready to watch an extremely important football game. By 6:45 they still had not appeared. I called and they told me that they received a call from me saying that I could not be at the house between those hours. I had made no such call to them and was at the house the entire three hours. I was going to miss the game. I did talk to a manager who sent someone to the house at 8:30 pm. They partially fixed the problem so I could watch the game, but they left me with incorrect information about why the cable was not performing as it should. Three days later I received the correct information from an excellent and reliable person, and the problems were resolved. Would you call the individual handling my initial call reliable? Absolutely not!

Another example: Imagine an employee who has a high collegiality rating, who is capable, but unreliable. This individual is involved in providing training seminars for the company but always puts off getting things done until the very last minute. He is not reliable, does not follow up with his work like he should on an ongoing basis, and at the very last moment, has to have a number of employees work until the wee hours of the morning to get his presentations ready.

To his credit, when everything is finished, he brings flowers in for those who worked to save him or takes them to lunch, etc. Still, everyone is tired of his lack of reliability. They do not find him so charming for failing to properly plan. They are not grateful that he frequently puts them under extreme pressure and stress.

To deal with this individual, he must be told that if he waits until the last moment again, the seminar will be canceled and he will be held accountable for it not being held. This is a case of an employee trying to substitute his charm through his very collegial personality for reliability, punctuality, and responsibility. The lesson here is that charm will get you though a problem once or twice, but once people realize it is habitual, charming is not so charming and becomes much less effective.

Another example involved Julie and Melissa. These two young women were the best of friends. They went to the same university, shared the same major, and even worked at the same restaurant as servers. One Memorial Day, they were both scheduled to work, but that particular morning was beautiful and the girls longed to spend it at the beach in Miami. They both called in sick to free up their day and drove to the beach for the day. The problem occurred when only one server showed up at the restaurant for a three-person shift. The result was horrific service to the customers and a fellow server who left in tears at the end of the day. The selfish and entitled attitude adopted by Julie and Melissa had consequences reaching far beyond their need for a day at the beach (RP).

Reliability in the workplace is extremely important to one's success. Your reputation, whether good or bad, follows you around as you develop your work life. Thus, from the beginning you want to cultivate a reputation as someone that people can count on. However, being reliable is not simply about getting the job done, rather it is also about doing the right thing.

Herbie, who served in World War II, had a 40-year career at General Motors. He retired to deliver and pick up laundry for a local cleaners and was the epitome of reliability. In one case, the cleaners ruined a woman's dress. The typical solution in this industry is for the cleaners to estimate the value of the dress and reimburse the customer—if it is the cleaner's fault. In this case, the cleaner did not accept responsibility immediately. Still, Herbie knew his customer and knew that this dress was one of the woman's favorites. So what did Herbie do? He went to the store where she bought it and found another just like it, purchased it and delivered it to woman. As this customer experienced, you could rely on Herbie to do the right thing! Oh, by the way, Herbie was 89 years old at the time. Be like Herbie! In this case, Herbie took it upon himself to maintain the customer and do what was right. Why? One, it makes good business sense. Two, Herbie had a relationship with the customer, and with that relationship he had the customer's trust. In this case, Herbie was going to do what was necessary to maintain that trust. What was the result? Herbie had a customer for life (RP).

Most people who have a reliability problem always have their reasons (excuses). It is easy to blame others for reliability failures. As stated in earlier chapters, we must face reality and take responsibility, not blame others. This is difficult for some people, as avoiding blame has become somewhat of the status quo in our society. We watch all day as people in government, celebrities, and even the people in our day-to-day lives duck and cover rather than stand up and face the consequences. The bigger problem is that they often get away with it. For this reason, we tend to adopt their behaviors, believing that we too can escape the consequences of our actions. While it would be misleading if I said it was not possible to avoid the consequences of our actions once or twice, the truth is that eventually your actions do catch up to you. The result is your disgrace and public damage to your reputation. The damage inflicted is often irreparable.

In contrast, you can take responsibility for your reliability and make yourself very successful—even when you have screwed up. Consider the following: Tom, a young man I once knew, had just gotten his driver's license. One night he was on his way home in a driving rain. Visibility was limited and Tom swerved off the road enough to clip a mailbox. Tom's truck was just fine, but the mailbox was destroyed. Now, in the driving rain and the middle of the night, nothing would have prevented Tom from simply driving away, but Tom did not. He knocked on the front door of the house, but nobody was home at the time. Undaunted, Tom left a note with his information and an apology for the incident. In the note, Tom also promised to make restitution for the mailbox.

When morning came, and the rain had passed, Tom got in his truck and went to the local hardware store where he bought a new mailbox. He then went back to the home where the incident took place and proceeded to replace the damaged mailbox himself. As he was finishing, the owner of the house arrived. Tom explained in detail what had happened and took responsibility for the incident, apologizing heavily. As it turned out, the owner of the house also owned an auto dealership in a neighboring town. He was so impressed with Tom's willingness to accept responsibility for his actions that he offered Tom a job on the spot in his service department. Tom accepted, and over the years his relationship with the owner blossomed. It has now been 20 years since Tom knocked down the mailbox—and now he owns that dealership (BW)!

Each of these chapters provides help on how to take charge of your work life and create greater success for yourself. You can liberate yourself by knowing how to be successful at work, which can greatly reduce stress in your life. For the best understanding, write out your answers to the following questions.

SELF ASSESSMENT

1. Would your colleagues say they can always count on you?
   Why or why not?_____
   _____
   _____
   _____
   _____

2. Are their often extenuating circumstances when you do
   not get something done on time? List some of the most
   common. _____
   _____
   _____
   _____
   _____

3. In the last six months have you missed a deadline for one
   reason or another? List your reasons here. Circle reasons
   which are duplicates _____
   _____
   _____
   _____
   _____
   _____

MY RELIABILITY CALCULATION

Where in my work can I show reliability?	My rating (1–5)	Importance to my work (Rate 1–5)	TOTAL SCORE

PERSONAL IMPROVEMENT PLAN

WEAKNESSES	CORRECTIVE ACTIONS	EXPECTED OUTCOMES

Bubba Can Dance

JOURNAL: HOW AM I DOING? *(IN YOUR OWN OPINION)*

1. _____

_____

_____

2. _____

_____

_____

3. _____

_____

_____

4. _____

_____

_____

5. _____

_____

_____

6. _____

_____

_____

TIPS:

- Start early and plan to finish early then you probably will always be done on time with high quality work.

- Do not bite off more than you can chew; i.e., do not take things on you cannot finish.

- Plan out your work and establish a timetable to get things done. Set progress checkpoints.

- Understand who you are working with and know their relationship and history of reliability.

- Always have a back-up plan for things that can go wrong.

CHAPTER 7

PERSISTENCE

Persistence can be defined as sticking with something until it gets done and done correctly. If you think back about learning a new skill, for example in sports—learning to play golf, tennis, pool, football, basketball, cricket, or learning to water or snow ski—you will remember, for most of us at least, how difficult it was at first. Learning individual aspects of each of these sports, to be able to perform them and then put them together can be quite difficult and tedious. The learning process takes considerable time and effort. Still, those who are willing to stick with it and persevere often become extremely competent, even masters. Winston Churchill said, "Success is not final, failure is not fatal. It is the courage to continue that counts."

To achieve any reasonable level of competence in any area requires not only talent, but also persistence. Persistence, that ability to keep finding ways to achieve what you want to achieve, or that others at work want you to achieve, is extremely critical to your success. In other words, *Never give up*.

A good example of lack of persistence that created major problems came when an employee, call him Bob, was asked to call three people to get their evaluations of a professional that the firm was about to engage in a contract to do a multi-year project. When asked about their three opinions, he responded, "The first person I called never called me back." Was Bob persistent? Of course not. What should he have done? He should have kept calling and also made sure that he was reachable when people called back.

On the other hand, Trevor, who works as a computer troubleshooter, was asked to see why my computer was acting up. Trevor was persistent, even though he kept getting seemingly stopped at every turn, unlike Bob, he kept with the problem until he figured it out and fixed the computer (RP)!

Think about the life of tennis player, Maria Sharapova. Maria was at the top of her game and number one in the world when she suffered a rotator cuff tear and lost her form. For most tennis players, this would have been the end of the road, but for Maria this simply represented a challenge—one she would rise to. After undergoing surgery and extensive rehabilitation, she literally had to re-learn the game of tennis. Many critics predicted that her career was over and that she would never play seriously again. Maria disagreed with their assessment and worked harder and longer than she ever had in order to regain her competitive edge. Today Maria finds herself in the hunt for the number one ranking again. She is a perfect example of a person being persistent. Never give up—and never listen to people who predict that you can't do something. If you want some inspiration about being persistent, just look to Maria (BW)!

Willie Nelson is another example of persistence that brings success. Born during the Great Depression and raised by his grandparents, Willie was writing and performing songs at a very early age. His first record was released in 1956 and he began to have some success, but, after mediocre results during the late 60s and early 70s, he retired from music. But shortly after retiring, he resumed his music career and, in the mid-70s, he had a number of hits.

During 1990 he had many of his assets seized by the IRS for back taxes due. He got through that and has gone on to become an American music icon. He has persisted through thick and thin to reach the top of his field. My father called this *stick-to-it-iveness*. I call it persistence (RP).

Take the example of NASCAR driver, Dale Earnhardt. Over the course of his career, Dale won seven Winston Cup Championships but after nineteen attempts one win alluded him: the Daytona 500. Year after year he would get close and then something would happen. His lack of success at Daytona would eventually become a leading story at every Daytona event. The pressure was immense, but Dale never made excuses for his lack of success. Rather, he kept working and working until he finally won the event in 1998 (BW).

Often, there are numerous challenges to getting something done at work. To achieve reliability and punctuality, show responsibility. You must use your knowledge and collegial relationships that you developed and get the job done right. Using all of these important facets will help you be persistent. Answer the following questions to better understand your own levels of persistence.

SELF ASSESSMENT

1. What projects, including those at work, home, or play, have you started and had to be persistent to get them done in the last year? _____

    _____

    _____

2. What projects including those at work, home, or play, have you started but did not finish? Why? _____

    _____

    _____

3. Do you give up easily? If so, why?_____

    _____

4. What discourages you the most when working on something? _____

    _____

5. How do you deal with discouragement?_____

    _____

6. Would you assess yourself as very persistent, somewhat persistent, or not very persistent? _____

    _____

7. Get an assessment from others. Ask your supervisor and fellow employees if they see you as very persistent, somewhat persistent, or not very persistent. Are you happy with their assessments?_____

MY PERSISTENCE CALCULATION

Where I need to be persistent in my work	My rating (1–5)	Importance to my work (Rate 1–5)	TOTAL SCORE

PERSISTENCE CALCULATION BY SUPERVISOR

Where I need to be persistent in my work	My rating (1–5)	Importance to my work (Rate 1–5)	TOTAL SCORE

PERSISTENCE CALCULATION BY COLLEAGUE 1

Where I need to be persistent in my work	My rating (1–5)	Importance to my work (Rate 1–5)	TOTAL SCORE

PERSISTENCE CALCULATION BY COLLEAGUE 2

Where I need to be persistent in my work	My rating (1–5)	Importance to my work (Rate 1–5)	TOTAL SCORE

PERSONAL IMPROVEMENT PLAN

WEAKNESSES	CORRECTIVE ACTIONS	EXPECTED OUTCOMES

JOURNAL: HOW AM I DOING? *(IN YOUR OWN OPINION)*

1. _____

_____

_____

2. _____

_____

_____

3. _____

_____

_____

4. _____

_____

_____

5. _____

_____

_____

6. _____

_____

_____

TIPS:

- Never give up!
- If you fail at first, try again (possibly with a new approach).
- Never let a lack of patience get the best of you.
- Things worth doing or accomplishing take persistence.
- Never get discouraged.
- Giving up is for quitters.
- Be realistic in your abilities before you take on a task. Should I challenge Eric Clapton to a guitar duel? I don't think so. You can't be persistent in getting something done that you don't have the skills, knowledge or aptitude to accomplish. But you *can* set about developing and acquiring the skills and knowledge you need.

Whoever is careless with the truth
in small matters cannot be trusted
with important matters.

—*Albert Einstein*

CHAPTER 8

HONESTY AND INTEGRITY

You may ask why we did not talk about this first. The reason is because most authors put it first, and most readers read it over quickly and assume that they know it is going to be the same old thing that has been said before, and then get on to the *real meat* of the other chapters. Instead, we wanted to put it later so that we can talk about it in more detail and you will benefit more from it.

In any organization, as in life, if you do not have honesty and integrity, over time you will lose out. In fact, if you are terribly dishonest and have no integrity, at some point you may lose it all. Remember a point we made earlier in the book: *Your reputation follows you around*. It is difficult, if not impossible, to hide from your past. Thus, you must preserve that reputation at all costs. It is, in many ways, your greatest asset.

Let's consider the example of Bernie Madoff. Bernie created a classic but massive Ponzi scheme, the largest in history. He bilked nearly $65 billion from investors. In a Ponzi scheme, the schemer takes money from investors for his own use but keeps enough available to pay early investors' returns on investments, as well as return their investment if requested, with the new money taken in on the scam. At some point in the scam there are not enough new funds coming in to meet those demands and the house of cards falls. In Madoff's case, the scam may have gone on for thirty years or more (RP).

Obviously the case of Bernie Madoff is a dramatic example of unethical behavior. So what does it take to be ethical? The answer is honesty, integrity, fairness and civility in dealing with others. It is where you set the bar for your proper behavior and treatment of others, it is your moral compass. In the workplace, it requires upholding the principles and values of the organization, being a good organizational citizen, and not committing deviant workplace behavior. The exception is when the organization is immoral. In other words, if you work for an organization that is unethical, don't succumb to their low standards—get out or blow the whistle! Why was Bernie Madoff able to convince so many people to invest with him? They thought he was honest and had integrity! For years, investors had received good returns with what appeared to be a very low risk.

Over time, given his results and the way he handled clients, he built up enormous trust. After a while, people who had come to trust him brought their friends, and the friends' trust of each other helped to calm questions concerning how Bernie got such great results. They thought, "He is just a genius!"

However, Bernie was not honest and had no integrity. This eventually destroyed his business, his family, his life, and the lives of many other people, including many charitable organizations.

He is spending the rest of his life in prison. He suffered a heart attack in December 2013 and is reported to be suffering from end-stage kidney cancer. There is a great deal of medical reasearch that demonstrates that not living in integrity will lead to illness.

Now let's consider the impact of having honesty and integrity. At some point in your life, you may have felt as if you were overcharged for your car's repair. Many people feel this way, as most of us have limited knowledge of mechanics of the modern automobile. Thus, when we take our car in for service, we are, in many ways, at the mercy of those with extensive knowledge. However, there are exceptions to the rule and one such exception was my grandfather, Wes Bills.

For many years my grandfather ran an auto repair service in a small town in southern Indiana. I knew he did good work, and we always took our cars to him for repairs when we could. I always remember the garage being dirty but filled with the cars of customers. My grandfather worked hard, put in long hours, and charged a reasonable price for his work. Eventually, he brought one of his sons and a grandson to work with him and taught them how he ran his business. However, I never knew the full extent of that business until he died.

My grandfather's viewing at the funeral home in his small home town was scheduled for four hours, and after eight hours people still had to be turned away who, in many cases, would come back the next day. I stood in awe at the multitude of people that my grandfather had interacted with. Most were customers whose cars he had serviced over the years. The stories were amazing, but they all had one common theme: My grandfather was an honest man of the highest integrity who did not lie, cheat, steal, or tolerate those who did. The result was that over time he became known throughout the community and the state as a man that could be counted on to be honest. People liked that, and they would often drive many miles—past hundreds of service stations—to get to my grandfather's shop. They knew he would treat them right. In some cases, I even met people who told me that he worked on their car for free when they did not have the money to pay him. They all eventually made good on their debts. It seems honesty brings out the best in people. In the end, people came from hundreds of miles away to pay their respects to a man they respected. His reputation had been well preserved, and he owed his success to it (BW).

This type of reputation develops over time. An important part of this is to be honest even when you think nobody is watching you—because you never know when they are! One such example involved a student I was teaching at Texas A&M University. I watched my student from afar one day as I was walking across campus. My student, whom I will call Matt, was just walking to class, following an older gentleman who was clearly a bit old to be an undergraduate. The old man appeared a bit turned around. When he stopped to check a campus map, he put down his briefcase. He was clearly in a hurry and when he continued on his way he accidentally left the briefcase behind. Matt noticed, grabbed the briefcase, and chased the man down to give it back to him.

Now, while this story is, on it surface, somewhat unremarkable, what happened later was. Later that day I ran into the older gentleman at the Association of Former Students on campus. I introduced myself and remarked that I had witnessed the briefcase incident earlier in the day. The old man smiled at me and remarked that it was actually quite fortunate that Matt had been so honest. "You see," he told me, "In that briefcase was over fifty thousand dollars in cash that I was donating to the university that day." I was stunned and greatly impressed, but not as impressed as the older gentleman. He was so impressed by Matt's integrity that he followed his academic career until graduation, and then offered him a six-figure job in his oil company. It seems integrity and honesty are valued and remembered (BW).

Living a life of integrity frees you from having to worry about lies. When you're honest, the right thing to do *is* what you do. To evaluate your own levels of honesty and integrity, consider and write out the answers to the following questions.

SELF ASSESSMENT

1. If you saw what you are doing written in the paper or shown on the news tomorrow would you be proud of it or ashamed of it? Why?_____

   _____

   _____

2. Is what you are doing fair to all involved? Why or why not?

   _____

   _____

   _____

3. Would you want to be treated like you are treating someone else? Why or why not? _____

   _____

   _____

   _____

4. Have you rationalized what you are doing to make it *seem right*? Why or why not? _____

   _____

   _____

MY HONESTY AND INTEGRITY CALCULATION

What are the top priorities for honesty and integrity in my work?	My rating (1–5)	Importance to my work (Rate 1–5)	TOTAL SCORE

PERSONAL IMPROVEMENT PLAN

WEAKNESSES	CORRECTIVE ACTIONS	EXPECTED OUTCOMES

Bubba Can Dance

JOURNAL: HOW AM I DOING? *(IN YOUR OWN OPINION)*

1. _____

_____

_____

2. _____

_____

_____

3. _____

_____

_____

4. _____

_____

_____

5. _____

_____

_____

6. _____

_____

_____

TIPS:

- Even if no one will ever know what you do—for better or worse—you will. When you do the right thing, you sleep better.

- When you live in integrity, your stress levels dramatically drop.

- When you encounter others who do not live in integrity, you have even greater reason to appreciate your own honesty.

- Remember that people are watching you and how you handle yourself. When you tell the truth in front of clients, colleagues, and children, then they know you are always truthful with them too (and vice versa).

- Treat your job as *your* business—as if you own the organization and the clients are all yours. Because you do and they are. If you own your job but you have no clients, you're out of business.

CHAPTER 9

PERSONAL LIFE

What does your personal life have to do with your success in the workplace? This is a little talked about subject that most consider to be taboo. However, the fact of the matter is that your personal life—what you do at home and/or away from the job—has a profound impact on your success at work. Once again, this book is written to help make you more successful at work. Be sure that you focus on YOU and your responsibilities at work. Do not focus on other people or their challenges while you are at work. Think of only yourself and your duties. To achieve that end, your personal life and activities outside the workplace must be evaluated.

Consider your life outside work. There are a great number of things in your personal life that can affect your work life, and probably do. If you stay out late during the week and then have to get up and go to work early the next day, you are tired and not really alert and ready to do your job. Your performance will not be up to par and your work will suffer—so will your success at work.

Do you drink alcohol to excess or do drugs? If you do, this clearly affects your success at work. It may even cause you to suddenly lose your job. If you have this problem, you need to seek help so that you do not fall into a downward spiral. Some who drink too much alcohol or moderately use drugs, say it is not a problem, "I just do it moderately for recreation and would never do it at work." Think again. Be honest with yourself. Are you really able to give it your all at work the next day after drinking a substantial amount of alcohol or using drugs? Would you pass a drug test?

Are you having significant problems with relatives that consume your time and emotions, causing you not to be able to concentrate on your work? Your home life may vary from being excellent, supportive, and motivating, to awful, destructive, and depressing. Depending on what you are facing at home, it is likely that there is significant carry over into your work life.

There is a great lesson in an old out-of-print Air Force officer's guide (one author read while in the Air Force in the 60s). An officer was asked to write about the biggest SOB he had ever met. He thought to himself I know the perfect SOB—John. As he began to write about John, he began to reflect on John and the fact that he had a very sick wife who required a lot of attention and had amassed huge medical bills. He wadded up the paper and threw it away.

Quickly he thought of another SOB—Bob—and he began to write about him. Then a similar thing happened. He remembered that Bob had a son who suffered from severe emotional and physical problems. He was always so worried about his boy that it probably made it seem that he was an SOB, so the officer threw away that piece of paper as well.

Finally, he thought of Tom and the officer was sure he had to be the world's biggest SOB. But soon he thought of Tom's family situation ,with Tom's sick elderly mother living with them, his wife out of work, and the bills piling up. At that point, a light went off in his head and he concluded there are no SOBs in the world—only people with problems (RP).

The real point of this chapter is to assess where you fall in the spectrum and what can be done to improve your personal problems, if necessary, so you can be more successful at work. These issues can become very complicated and require professional help that is beyond the scope of this book.

Also, your company's human resources department may be able to refer you to the proper professionals, or if your firm has an Employee Assistant Program (EAP), that is a good place to go for assistance with these matters. On the other hand, if the problems are mild, you can solve them by creating your own coping mechanisms.

If there are issues outside of work within your control that are impacting the way that you perform on the job, it is *your responsibility* to control those issues and make the necessary adjustments outside of work to maintain your performance on the job. However, you may have also noted that most of the examples highlighted here concern problems at home which may not be entirely within the control of the employees involved.

In many cases, you find yourself in life situations that impact your work that you did not create. What makes these situations difficult is that you are incapable of making immediate changes that *just make them go away.* Consider the following.

Robert's family owns a small business in a small town. His parents are in their sixties and pushing retirement. Their life has been their business and the income that they drew from it. They planned to sell the business when they retired to ease the financial burden that retirement often brings. However, before selling the property, they learned that a property adjacent to theirs had a significant pollution problem caused by a petroleum spill. The contamination had leaked onto their property and made its sale impossible. Robert, being the dutiful son, stepped in to help his parents with the lawsuit and the years of cleanup mandated by the government. As a result, Robert spent long hours researching the problem and writing countless letters on his parent's behalf to state officials and various attorneys. Those long hours began to significantly impact his work performance on the job. He was tired. He was stressed. And worst of all, the process of getting his parents out of this mess looked to have no end in sight.

Now, naturally Robert is not simply going to just walk away from his parents. Still, he has a job to do and supervisors that are starting to notice that his performance is on the decline. What should he do? The answer may startle you a bit. However if we look to the examples provided earlier in this chapter, the answer, in part, becomes self evident. The first thing Robert has to do is become transparent.

Robert's supervisor has no idea what is going on in his life at home. The only thing that the supervisor knows is that there is work to be done, and that the work must be completed on time and with a high level of quality. Without some form of communication from Robert, the supervisors will remain in the dark and will judge him based on performance alone without regard to anything that may be driving that performance—or lack of it. To that end, it becomes Robert's duty to explain the situation at home to his boss.

Doing so allows for several good things to happen: 1) Robert's boss develops an understanding of what is driving his performance decline, thus allowing the boss to be a bit more understanding. 2) Robert's boss can now help Robert by offering help, work redesign, and workflow assistance until Robert gets back on his feet. 3) By working with his superiors and disclosing his personal situation, Robert demonstrates to his superiors that he is fully committed to the job and to his performance (BW).

The key here, and something that we will discuss further in the chapter on communication, is that the boss has to be told. Supervisors do not know what is going on in your lives unless you tell them. When you face situations that will impact your work performance, the boss needs to be told early so that understanding can be cultivated. Further, another key to success with this strategy is that Robert does not have a history of chronic excuses making for poor performance. If that were the case, his family situation would likely be looked at as just *another* excuse for Robert failing.

One final word on Robert and his parents: It should be noted here that I have some personal experiences that line up with Robert's. I have lived out this scenario to some degree, and I know the importance of self-assessment. If you face a situation like Robert's, you must make an effort to constantly assess your needs (personal and professional) and fight to maintain a balance. Robert can't do much for his parents if he loses his job, yet his job will be harder if he fails his parents. Thus, Robert has to work to maintain a balance between the two, allowing him to perform on both fronts.

This requires Robert to constantly self-assess his performance honestly in order to maintain that balance (BW).

Brooke Shields said, "The thing I'm the most proud of in my personal life is that my daughter actually thinks that I'm fabulous." You will know you have done well maintaining balance in your personal life when your children, siblings, or parents say such a thing about you.

To evaluate how your personal problems affect your career, consider and write out the answers to the following questions.

SELF ASSESSMENT

1. Are you alert and ready for work each day?_____
   If not, why not? Do alcohol, drugs, or sleep deprivation
   have a role in the situation? _____

   _____
   _____
   _____

2. If you have significant family problems with your spouse,
   children, or others, what will you tell your boss about
   them?_____

   _____
   _____
   _____

3. If you have hobbies or other interests that greatly distract
   you from your work, list them here and include them in
   your improvement plan. _____

   _____
   _____
   _____

MY PERSONAL LIFE CALCULATION

When does my personal life affect my work?	My rating (1–5)	Importance to my work (Rate 1–5)	TOTAL SCORE

PERSONAL IMPROVEMENT PLAN

WEAKNESSES	CORRECTIVE ACTIONS	EXPECTED OUTCOMES

JOURNAL: HOW AM I DOING? *(IN YOUR OWN OPINION)*

1. _____
_____
_____

2. _____
_____
_____

3. _____
_____
_____

4. _____
_____
_____

5. _____
_____
_____

6. _____
_____
_____

Bubba Can Dance

TIPS:

- Do not let the leisure part of your personal life interfere with work.

- If your organization has an Employee Assistance Program (EAP), use it if needed.

- If you are in a relationship that is problematic, seek help.

- If you consume alcohol, do so in moderation.

- Do not do drugs. If you do, seek help immediately.

- Always remember the importance of transparency when dealing with significant personal challenges.

You are not here merely to make a living.
You are here in order to enable the world to live
more amply, with greater vision,
with a finer spirit of hope and achievement.

You are here to enrich the world,
and you impoverish yourself if you forget the errand.

—*Woodrow Wilson*

　　　　　　　　　Bubba Can Dance

CHAPTER 10

VISION

What do you want for your life or lifestyle? Where do you want to be with regard to wealth, job security, free time, hobbies, etc., now and in five, ten, or fifteen years? In other words, do you have a vision of where you are going with your life and a plan for how you're going to get there?

Some people want work to have a major significance in their lives. They want to be secure in their jobs and accumulate funds for a good retirement. Other people are not focused on their jobs. They are consumed by other activities. They often live from paycheck to paycheck, and do not really care about security at the end of their lives. Take the time to consider what level of security you prefer and how you're going to create it for yourself.

Take the time to look at your current position on the scale for your future vision. The low end has you not caring about your job at all, or your future, or your job security. The other end of the scale has you caring about your job, your future, your job security.

You are also looking at your longevity and have retirement plans.

I am not asking if you have a well-thought out, documented (written) strategic plan for your future. That is not it at all. I would say that 99.9% of the people do not have a master plan of this sort. The question is have *you* thought about where you want to be in your life, where are you going, when you intend to be there, and what you desire regarding your success in life? Do you have the drive and determination to get something done and make something happen for yourself?

Let's take a look at two polar examples. The first example is a brief summary of the H. Wayne Huizenga story. Mr. Huizenga went to college for a short time and then joined the Army reserve. After his service, he started working for his uncle as a garbage collector. That certainly was not what Mr. Huizenga wanted to do when he came back from the Army, but very quickly he began to see this could be a successful business. He borrowed $5,000 and bought his own garbage truck. He and his brother-in-law would get up early each morning and pick up the garbage. Then they would come home at midday, take a shower, put on a shirt, pants, and tie, and go out and sell more garbage routes.

Mr. Huizenga did not have a vision of one day being the head of a multi-million dollar company, but he did have the drive, determination and vision to see he was onto something. As a result, he went on to create Waste Management, which, in 1981, reached sales of $772 million as the world's largest garbage company.

He then went on to build Blockbuster Video and sold it for $8.4 billion. From there he created AutoNation and was involved in setting up Extended Stay America. Mr. Huizenga did not have a gigantic master plan laying out every step for the next ten years, but he had the vision, drive, determination, and the desire to make something happen. Mr. Huizenga also embodied all the other attributes discussed in the chapters of this book.

Now let us take a look at another individual named Don. Every time Don took a new job, he was going to dominate it within a short period of time and run his segment of the business. He always had grandiose visions of where he would be in a very short time. They were not based in reality and not attainable without more time, training, greater skill levels, and the other factors in this book. Don never reached his major goals and became discouraged. Worse, he always rationalized that it was someone else's fault when he didn't end up with the corner office and the private jet. The result was a never-ending spiral of failures and missed opportunities.

Unfortunately, Don did not have the realistic vision to know where he could go over time nor what it would take to get there. There is a difference between having a vision and simply dreaming about where you would like to be in the future. He was unrealistic in his dreams—he did not plan for them, he did not have the drive, or the determination, and he did not have a strong work ethic. Further, he did nothing to change that, choosing instead to blame others when he failed. He was not willing to get the training, education, and knowledge necessary to take on his dreams. Plus, his collegial skills were not adequate enough for him to reach his vision. He did not really have a vision. He just had an unrealistic dream of where he wanted to be in the future (BW).

There is a big difference between a vision and determination to get where you want to be. There is a difference between working hard to achieve your goal as opposed to simply daydreaming about having a lot of money and a big job in the future. The differences come from honest self-assessment and a willingness to make changes necessary in order to reach those big dreams.

Another example comes from Josh Rowand, the leader of the *Pitbull of Blues Band* that I frequently sit in with. Rowand is a world class guitarist, musician, and entertainer. He has said, as have many others I have jammed with (including my high school guitar hero and now close friend Nokie Edwards, former lead guitar player for the *Ventures*), "If you had been playing as much as I have over the years, you would be just as good on the guitar."

Not so! Many, many years ago I was honest enough with myself to admit I had much more talent in other areas than I did playing the guitar, so I focused my attention and energy on creating a very successful career in business and academics. It took me many years to realize that people have gifts and some gifts are extordinary. Sure *Bubba Can Dance,* and you can too—but be realistic. If you set your goals such that you cannot hope to reach them, you will live a life of disappointment. Make sure that your dream has a life beyond your imagination by creating a plan to make it happen and following that plan. Have a realistic vision based on your abilities, as well as the world around you. You don't jump to the top rung of the ladder from the ground floor. You climb (RP).

It should be noted that there is nothing wrong with having a grand vision of your future—most successful people do. However, the difference between achieving your dreams, and not, falls on you and your ability to assess yourself. Do you have what you need to put yourself on a path to success? If not, you have nobody to blame but yourself.

Bubba Can Dance

Each one of these chapters is integrated with the other chapters. When thinking about your vision for your future, you must consider all of the things we have addressed to this point. What kind of knowledge and skills do you have that would allow you to go to the next level of an organization? Do you take on responsibility? Do you try to expand what you are capable of doing and take responsibility no matter what and who is actually responsible? Do you make sure the job gets done? Are you punctual? Are you always at work on time? Do you get projects done on time? Would your supervisor and colleagues call you punctual? Are you collegial? Do you communicate well? Are you the kind of person that others want to work with? Are you persistent in getting your job done and doing it right? Do you have honesty and integrity? Is your personal life in order so that it is not causing serious problems?

In each chapter, as you build on integrating each behavior and quality, you must also consider how the previous chapter topics have an impact on the current chapter and your plan. Consider the following questions and write out your answers.

SELF ASSESSMENT

1. Describe in detail your vision for something better for yourself in the workplace._____

   _____

   _____

   _____

   _____

   _____

2. Why is this your vision? _____

   _____

   _____

3. What will it take to realize your vision?_____

   _____

   _____

4. What am I willing to do differently to get there? What do I have to add? What do I have to give up? _____

   _____

   _____

   _____

5. How long will it take?_____

6. How do you know you have the desire, determination, and drive to get there? _____

   _____

   _____

MY VISION CALCULATION

Why is vision important to my work?	My rating (1–5)	Importance to my work (Rate 1–5)	TOTAL SCORE

PERSONAL IMPROVEMENT PLAN

WEAKNESSES	CORRECTIVE ACTIONS	EXPECTED OUTCOMES

Bubba Can Dance

JOURNAL: HOW AM I DOING? *(IN YOUR OWN OPINION)*

1. _____

_____

_____

2. _____

_____

_____

3. _____

_____

_____

4. _____

_____

_____

5. _____

_____

_____

6. _____

_____

_____

TIPS:

- Study the lives of people you admire and want to be like.

- Whichever lifestyle you prefer, whether it is the life of the rich and famous, Bohemian lifestyle, or somewhere in between, savor all the best it has to offer.

- Write out your plan for getting where you want to be in one, three, five, ten, and twenty years. Dream big but to get real results, your plan must be real.

- Set up steps (milestones) to get there within the time frame.

- Work with focus and determination to meet every milestone.

- Never underestimate yourself.

CHAPTER 11

COMMUNICATION

I hear these questions every day:

What can we do to enhance communication here?

Why do my employees have such a problem with communication?

Why won't my boss just talk to me?

Communication has become a hallmark issue in the modern business world, and it seems that everyone has problems with it. The problem is that, when it comes to communication, we know so much that *just isn't so*. Too often, we accept assumptions as fact.

The first assumption that you make is that you are good at communicating. After all, you have all been doing it since you were born. You got hungry, cried, and got a bottle. You had a need, screamed about it, and someone met the need. Simple right?

As you wandered through the world, you communicated in one way or another every day, so, by the time you are 25, you should be good at it right? Well, not really. The problem really started with that first communication as a baby. You had a need, screamed, and the need was met. From that point on you kind of assumed that since your mom knew what you wanted at that moment, everyone else on the planet must understand you as well in every moment. They get you, right? Wrong.

Communication is a skill that must be developed and practiced over time in order to become proficient at it. Notice that I said *proficient* and not *perfect*. You will never get it right all the time. I have a PhD in communication, and I still have my struggles. However, by working at it, you can improve greatly. You do not have to be stuck with poor communication skills, but you do have to recognize the need for improvement.

I once had a boss we will call Dawn. Dawn was an older woman who liked to yell at employees and, at times, berate them in public. She insisted in interacting with me in the same way. The problem in this case is that she had a communication style that had long worked for her and produced results. Thus, she had no desire to approach the subject differently. Then she met me.

Even as a child I knew that I simply do not respond well to people yelling at me. I get stressed out and that stress sometimes leads to rash action and mistakes. My dealings with Dawn were no different. She would yell at me and I would stress out. This led to errors, which caused her to yell even more.

We had a horrible relationship, and I saw no way to fix it. I was worried that she hated me and would eventually fire me. As the months went on, I progressively became more unhappy in the job. Dawn's relationship with me continued to deteriorate until finally I arrived at a decision to either quit or try something radical.

I decided on the radical. After all, what did I have to lose? I set a meeting with Dawn in a conference room where we could speak in private. I will never forget the rage in her eyes as she arrived at the meeting, shut the door and barked, "What's the meaning of this?"

I looked her straight in the eye and, in a calm and deliberate voice, explained that I thought that we had a communication problem. I explained that I had not done well with being yelled at since I was a child. I suggested that in order to improve my performance, we would have to figure out a way to communicate with each other more productively. The next few minutes passed in a blur as I told her the best way to communicate with me in order to enhance my productivity and get what she wanted from me as an employee, just by making a few changes in how we communicate. The whole time Dawn sat in silence.

When I was done talking Dawn looked at me and said something totally unexpected. She said, "Brad, I am so sorry—I had no idea." We then discussed the matter a bit further and eventually collaborated on a new way that we would interact. The results were dramatic. I kept my job, was happier, and even came to call Dawn a friend.

So what happened here? In this situation, Dawn and I were at a communication impasse. I assumed that she knew how to manage everyone because—well—she was a manager. She assumed that the communication style that she had used with success in the past would work for anyone. We were both wrong. However, had I not initiated the conversation with her, we might well have parted company without ever realizing it (BW).

As a consultant I often deal with employees who tell me

horrifying things about their bosses. This boss is mean. That boss does not care about my situation. The boss over there simply is clueless about what I do in my job. In each of these, I often ask the employee a question that makes them think. "Have you ever told your boss that you feel this way?" The question is almost always answered with some version of "no". The most common responses include the assumption that the boss should already know about it. Really? When did bosses become all knowing beings?

The point here is that I encourage employees at all levels to open the lines of communication. You cannot assume that your boss knows everything going on in your life unless you communicate with them. Further, when you become a manager, never lose sight of the fact that your employees need to know what is happening in your professional and personal world if they are going to adapt and perform well for you. In short, self-disclosure becomes a real key.

In this book, we have talked about a great many subjects from acquiring skills to establishing a realistic vision for success. I assure you that open communication with your superiors is a key to success for each behavior and skill. Take visioning for example. I once knew a lady who had worked as an executive assistant quite successfully for a number of years. She was outstanding at her job, but she had bigger dreams of running the informatics segment of the business, as this was the area her interest and college degree. Her boss (who was the CEO and could have made her dream a reality) never promoted her, and eventually this led her to a point at which she was considering quitting and moving on.

When she came to me for advice she spoke of her boss as cold, disconnected, and uninterested in her advancement. So, I asked her my question, "Have you ever told you boss that you feel this way?" She looked at me quizzically and laughed, but I told her that her boss probably had no idea of her vision for her career if she had not told him. In the end, she took my advice out of desperation. If she was going to quit anyway, why not lay her position on the line with the boss?

When she had the meeting, her boss was astounded. He had *no idea* of her aspiration, her vision, or even the fact that she had attained her degree in informatics. In the end, he asked for a bit more time to find a position for her and find a replacement. She moved to her dream position in informatics a month later and now runs the entire department. The point is that having a vision is not worth a thing if you do not communicate that vision to those who can help you achieve it (BW).

The goal here is for you to think about how you communicate or even if you do it at all. If you are unhappy at work, chances are you blame your boss a lot. If so, ask yourself, "Have I ever told my boss how I feel?" If the answer is *no,* you cannot expect your boss to magically make things better for you. The boss has no idea what is going on unless you tell them.

One other interesting facet of my profession is that I often work with people at the management or executive level. When the subject of communication comes up, I often get a consistent complaint. Managers everywhere agree that they wish that there was some way to make their employees talk to them—REALLY talk to them.

In other words, bosses everywhere wish that they knew more of what they could do to make their reports better and more productive. Think about that for a moment. Your boss—right now—would love to have a frank conversation with you about what you need to be successful. So, what's stopping you from communicating with them?

Ronald Reagan said, "I've always believed that a lot of the trouble in the world would disappear if we were talking to each other instead of about each other." You've got to talk *to* the person you have trouble with for them to know you have the trouble. Telling everyone else does no good whatsoever, except to make you feel frustrated and unheard.

Communication is not just something that happens without our thinking about it. In fact, we have to think of it often and we have to work at it constantly. Often non-verbal communication sends clearer messages than words. I counsel undergraduates who are seeking jobs about what their appearance communicates to future employers. Students are often shocked to find out what wrinkled slacks, an improperly tied necktie, or a dress that is too revealing says to their potential employers. They discover that their every action communicates something and that, through controlling their actions, they can also control the message that is being sent. The fun part for me is watching small changes make such a big difference in the way that employers view them.

The goal of this chapter is to get YOU to think about the messages that you are sending, or not sending. What are you saying to those around you? When was the last time you really *talked* to your boss? When was the last time you really *talked* to the people that work for you? Consider the following questions and write out your answers.

SELF ASSESSMENT

1. If you are having problems with your boss, write here what you plan to say when you tell them how you feel. _____

    _____

    _____

    _____

2. Describe a situation in which you know you were a great communicator._____

    _____

    _____

3. Who is the best communicator that you know and what characteristics can you adopt that make them successful?

    _____

    _____

    _____

4. How do you know that your boss knows what you want? _

    _____

    _____

5. Listening is a key element of communication. Describe the difference when you are listening to respond and when you are listening to understand. _____

    _____

    _____

    _____

MY COMMUNICATION CALCULATION

Why is communication important to my work?	My rating (1–5)	Importance to my work (Rate 1–5)	TOTAL SCORE

PERSONAL IMPROVEMENT PLAN

WEAKNESSES	CORRECTIVE ACTIONS	EXPECTED OUTCOMES

JOURNAL: HOW AM I DOING? *(IN YOUR OWN OPINION)*

1. _____

_____

_____

2. _____

_____

_____

3. _____

_____

_____

4. _____

_____

_____

5. _____

_____

_____

6. _____

_____

_____

TIPS:

- Self-assess your relationship with your boss and resolve to open communication.

- Set a quarterly meeting with your boss so that you can express new concerns and hear your supervisor's opinion.

- If you determine that you have significant problems with expressing yourself, seek the help of a professional consultant.

- Work extremely hard to enhance communication at all levels of your organization.

- Never assume that you are a *perfect* communicator and resolve to work at it all your life.

Nothing can stop the man with the right mental attitude
from achieving his goal; nothing on earth can
help the man with the wrong mental attitude.

—Thomas Jefferson

———

The greatest day in your life and mine is when
we take total responsibility for our attitudes.
That's the day we truly grow up.

—John C. Maxwell

CHAPTER 12

ATTITUDE

Last, but not least, we must discuss attitude. My guess is that you have already been thinking about this during the reading of the previous chapters. What do we mean by *attitude*? You might not be able to give a precise definition, or put it into words exactly, but we all know what we mean when we discuss someone's attitude in a work context.

Attitude affects everything you do at work, home, or play. Your attitude is created first by how you perceive something. When something takes place, do you choose to see it as something that is impacting you in a good or bad way? Second, how does it affect you? How do you feel about it? Did it make you angry, happy, sad, etc.? Third, how do you react to the first two elements, and behave as a result of this? This is typically how *attitude* is viewed in the workplace.

After a person has had more experience, they tend to create a pattern for how they see, feel, and behave. This pattern creates an overall characteristic of the person which we call the *attitude*. Think of it as a general way of dealing with the world. In other words, you get programmed to see, feel, and behave in a certain way over time, and that programming shapes your experiences.

You develop an overall attitude over time due to the way you have grown up with your family, and your personal religious, work, cultural, and play experiences. You create a way of seeing the world, or perceptual frame of reference—in other words—your overall attitude. You have often heard the phrase, "Is the cup half empty or half full?" Those who see the cup as half empty have a more negative attitude toward life, and those who see the glass as half full, see an opportunity in everything. Which attitude do you have? Where you don't see opportunity, there is no motivation to proceed.

An important concept here is that your attitudes are not set in stone. You CAN change them.

Nothing is more annoying than people who pretend that their lot in life, where they are from, or what they have experienced, has somehow preconditioned them to be a nasty mean person that nobody gets along with. That is hogwash! While we are all affected by our past, the way we approach anything today is a conscious choice that we make now.

If you tend to think of the *glass* at work as being half empty all the time, you have to ask yourself *why?* If you always leave staff meetings thinking that the new idea or new procedure is not going to work, you must consider why that is. Is it that the idea is bad or is it just that you have allowed yourself to approach everything negatively?

The good news with regard to changing your attitude is that it

IS within your locus of control to do so. The first step is knowing that you have developed a negative attitude. Once you know it, you will become keenly more aware of the times that you become negative in your daily life. Recognizing these times allows you to do something about it.

Therapists have known for years that a major part of dealing with patients' depression is simply getting them to recognize when they are triggered into a downward spiral and then giving them the tools to stop and get out of it. The process involves recognition of the trigger and then a conscious effort to deal with the trigger, rather than embracing the negativity. While it sounds simplistic, it *is* just that easy. Once negative tendencies are identified, control is regained. When you feel yourself going negative, you can ask why you are feeling that way. In the absence of a logical reason, you can then choose to approach the subject in a more positive light.

I love to eat, and, on occasion, I really love going out to high-end restaurants. In my life I have been lucky enough to eat all over the country, and I have noticed that there are major differences in attitude among restaurant servers. One of my favorite restaurants is a high-end seafood chain. The food is always wonderful and makes for a great dining experience. However, the servers are not always as consistent.

While in Miami a few years, ago my wife and I went out to dinner and were stunned by the server's bad attitude. He was rude, pompous, did not smile, and was generally sloppy. He clearly did not want to be at work or serving us dinner. In the end, I went to his manager about his service.

This led to an interesting conversation with the manager in which he disclosed that he had received numerous complaints about the server—and, in fact, about several of their servers—over the past few months. The result was more than a few unsatisfied patrons. Not too surprisingly, the servers were complaining of having trouble surviving on small tips.

At the end of the conversation I was concerned by the manager's perception that attitude was something that was unchangeable. He seemed to think that his servers were incapable of changing their attitude and that the solution was to simply hire new servers. I offered him my services and he hired me to come work with his staff.

I returned a week later to meet with the servers. The meeting was eye opening. The servers explained that because Miami was a tourist city, patrons often treated them poorly—as if they were servants rather than servers. This happened so frequently that the servers had come to expect bad behavior from patrons even before they arrived at the table. Thus, because they always felt that they would be treated poorly, the servers made almost no effort at providing quality service with a positive attitude.

The challenge for the group was embracing two important facts: 1) They could not control their customer's attitude—only their own, and 2) Attitudes are contagious.

The first step for the servers was learning that they could only control themselves. If their customers were having a bad day or were just rude, it was out of their hands. However, attitudes (positive and negative) impact those around us. Others often pick up on our attitude, especially if it is strong and pervasive. Combining both of these facts, I challenged the servers to approach each customer, regardless of that customer's disposition at the time they arrived, with a smile and a positive attitude that they controlled. The challenge, of course, would be in staying positive if the customer was not. However, I informed them that if they did stay positive, the customer would likely eventually lighten up. The servers were skeptical but agreed to try. I followed up in two weeks and, without exception, the servers reported that the work environment had improved, as had their relationships with customers. Even more important to the servers—gratuities has increased threefold (BW).

The point here, once again, is one of self-assessment combined with controlling what you, as an employee, *can* control. By doing so, you can spawn positivity in those with whom you interact. You can also foster a positive attitude in those around you.

You have heard someone say, "Boy, does she have an attitude!" You know you have your own values, attitudes, opinions, and beliefs generated through your experiences. How do all of these create your overall attitude? How does it affect your success in the workplace? The answer is: Drastically!

Your overall attitude has an impact at work and affects all other areas discussed in this book. It is critical that you do an honest self assessment improvement plan, and keep an accurate journal. Consider these questions and write out your answers.

SELF ASSESSMENT

1. Do you see the glass as half empty or half full most of the time? Why do you feel it is an accurate point of view? ___
    _____
    _____

2. Do you have an internal or external locus of control most of the time? What if it was reversed? _____
    _____
    _____

3. Do you have a good or a bad attitude about life and work most of the time? Describe how changing your attitude has changed a situation for you. _____
    _____
    _____
    _____

4. Ask yourself why you have the internal or external locus of control or why you see the glass as half empty or half full. Would your colleagues say that you have a good or bad attitude about life and work? Be as honest and detailed as possible. _____
    _____
    _____
    _____
    _____
    _____

MY COMMUNICATION CALCULATION

In what ways can my attitude affect my work?	My rating (1–5)	Importance to my work (Rate 1–5)	TOTAL SCORE

PERSONAL IMPROVEMENT PLAN

WEAKNESSES	CORRECTIVE ACTIONS	EXPECTED OUTCOMES

Bubba Can Dance

JOURNAL: HOW AM I DOING? *(IN YOUR OWN OPINION)*

1. _____

_____

_____

2. _____

_____

_____

3. _____

_____

_____

4. _____

_____

_____

5. _____

_____

_____

6. _____

_____

_____

TIPS

- Next time someone asks "How are you?" stop what you're doing, look them in the eyes, answer with enthusiasm and say, "Marvelous! How are you?" Watch their response.

- Your self-talk defines a lot of your attitude. Look yourself in the mirror each morning as you dress and declare what a great day you're going to have.

- Expect wonderful things to happen.

- Place printed affirmations around you in your environment, including at home, in your car, and on your personal phone. You can find these on social media sites as well as our website, www.Bubba-Can-Dance.com. Choose your favorites and print them out. Share them with friends.

- Never again say, "I'm tired." Instead, say, "I have gotten so much accomplished!" Your words affect your body, emotions and mindset.

CHAPTER 13

CONCLUSION

This book has one objective: to help YOU be more successful in the workplace. This book is for YOU, not anyone else. This will translate into a better personal life, reduce work-related stress, and result in greater compensation in job security over time. This book is not for your boss, friends, or family. It is for you to personally evaluate your various attributes and how they can be positively modified to make you more successful at work. You will get better results if this book and your notes are private so you can self-evaluate honestly, and not worry about what others think.

We have covered the importance of knowledge, responsibility, punctuality, collegiality, honesty, integrity, persistence, personal life, communication, vision, and attitude for your workplace success. Now your job is to make sure you honestly do your self-evaluations, set up behavioral improvement plans and keep an accurate journal of your successes and failures so you can get better each day.

YOU are the master of your destiny. YOU must be patient and keep working to improve your behavior. While some areas will not need much improvement, other areas may be quite challenging. The process may be like losing weight or stopping smoking. You might take two steps forward, and one step back, but remain aware and determined to improve your behaviors and enhance your success in the workplace. Remember the eleven behaviors of workplace winners:

- KNOWLEDGE: What do you know about your workplace and can you apply that knowledge effectively?

- RESPONSIBILITY: Do you take full responsibility for work being done on time with high quality?

- PUNCTUALITY: Are you at work on time? Do you finish your work on time?

- COLLEGIALITY: Are you friendly at work? Do people want to work with you and get your ideas and appreciate you as a good colleague?

- PERSISTENCE: Are you like a junk yard dog and never give up? Do you get the job done, and done right, no matter what?

- RELIABILITY: Can your employer count on you to get the job done and do the right thing?

- HONESTY and INTEGRITY: Are you honest in your dealings with others in the workplace? Do you do you say you will do?

- PERSONAL LIFE: Is your personal life in order? Does it create a distraction to you being successful in the workplace?

- COMMUNICATION: How open is your communication with those around you? What can you do to enhance communication at every level of your organization?

- VISION: Where are you going with your life, and how does work fit into that?

- ATTITUDE: Is the glass half empty or half full? Do you have an external or internal locus of control? Do you have a good or bad attitude?

Now, it is up to you. You are the master of your destiny. You can make it happen and can be incredibly successful in the workplace. Make it fun. Look at this as a play that you're not only living, you're writing, starring in, and casting. If you don't like the way the story is unfolding, create something better! You are the only one creating your life, so make it into something you really enjoy. But, you have to put forth the best you've got to be the best you can be.

Some final advice:

- Make it fun
- Be patient
- Persistence pays off
- Relish your personal successes
- Do not get discouraged and
- Best of luck to you!

THE END—of the book but the beginning of your success!

Bubba Can Dance

About the Authors

RANDY POHLMAN, PH.D.

Dr. Randolph A. Pohlman is Dean Emeritus and Professor at Nova Southeastern University. His undergraduate, Masters and Ph.D. have all emphasized Finance and Organizational Behavior. He served in the United States Air force as an officer after receiving his Masters degree.

After his Ph.D., he went to Kansas State University, his alma mater, in a faculty position, then to UCLA in 1983 as a visiting research scholar, returning the following year to become the dean at Kansas State.

In 1990, he went to Koch Industries as a senior executive, which had a major impact in solidifying his beliefs in the importance of successful work and its impact on ones life. Dr. Pohlman has an extensive consulting and research background.

He lives with his wife Jeanne and has two daughters: Tina Pohlman and Lisa Bergeron. Lisa and her husband, Adam, have given Dr. Pohlman and his wife two wonderful grandsons: Zach and Mike. Dr. Pohlman is an avid golfer. He is also a blues guitar player and singer, also known as *BigBuick* with *BigBuick and The Roadmasters*, and can often be seen jamming with the *Pitbull of Blues Band*.

NOTE: If you are a guitar player and wonder what guitar I am playing in the picture above, it is a HitchHiker, made by my friend Nokie Edwards. You can find him at *www.nokieedwards.com.*

BRADLEY WESNER, PH.D.

Dr. Bradley Wesner is a leadership, communication, and teamwork specialist at Sam Houston State University. Brad's Bachelor's Degree was in Criminology and he worked as a law enforcement officer for several years in Indianapolis before making a transition into the insurance industry. As an insurance settlement specialist, Brad was instrumental in revolutionizing settlement practices for CNA Insurance and AIG, where he developed a process for settlement of long term disability and worker's compensation claims. After working to train individuals within those organizations on the new practice, he decided to return to advance his education and pursue his PhD. After receiving his Master's degree in Applied Communication through Indiana University in 2007, he pursued and received his PhD from Texas A&M University in 2011.

Brad has extensive experience in working with teams and teamwork and has focused on development of high performance teams and rapid resilience practices with his current body of research focusing on those topics. Brad has served as a trainer and consultant for a variety of profit and non-profit organizations including Univision and Heico Corporation, and is known for his dynamic training style and ability to make complex theory understandable and applicable to the modern business organization.

He lives with his wife Kylene, daughter Anastasia, and Golden Retriever Maggie in College Station, Texas and is an avid fisherman and French chef in his spare time. Find him on Facebook at facebook.com/KBOConsulting and Twitter @bswesner.

ENDNOTES

ENDNOTES

ENDNOTES

ENDNOTES

ENDNOTES

ENDNOTES

www.ingramcontent.com/pod-product-compliance
Lightning Source LLC
Chambersburg PA
CBHW051707170526
45167CB00002B/571